One Carry-On Item

Hannah Adams

Copyright © 2020 Hannah Adams

Published by Cliff Street Books

All rights reserved. For information, contact Cliff Street Books. CliffStreetBooks@ithacajosh.com

ISBN: 0578710594
ISBN-13: 978-0-578-71059-4

Cover Art by Gabrielle Maye
gabriellemaye.com

Cover Design by Joshua Adams

First Paperback Printing: June 2020
Printed in the United States of America

Library of Congress Control Number: 2020911596

For the backpackers

This book is the accumulation of poetry written during my time living and traveling abroad. In 2011, I moved from Philly, PA to New Delhi, India for university studies. After college, I lived and worked in Brazil, India, Guatemala, and Peru, eventually moving back to my hometown of Boston, MA. These poems are inspired by my travels, relationships, and worldview during those years.

I hope you'll relate to the feelings and perspectives shared, and allow these poems to take you on a journey!

Contents

Writing Right 1
Culture Shock 3
Restless 4
The Places I've Prayed 5
Why I Didn't Write Home 6
Hopeful Romantic 8
The Travelers 9
Think About It 10
Cup of Tea 11
Express Train 13
Killing Time 14
Pack light 16
Dear Tomek 17
Brother 20
Missing Out 21
Shipwreck 22
Queso Fresco and Paneer 23
Roxanne 24
Backpackers 26
Felipe 28
Maracuja 30
Orange You Glad 32
Hangry 34
Recipe for Disaster 35

A Good Find	38
11,000 feet	39
Sacred Space	41
Go	43
Moving On	44
The Rush	46
Allow	47
Love Me	48
Affirmation	51
Lake Water Calm	52
Loving Me	53
The Hum of Home	55
Mourning Walks	58
Forever 21	62
Red Eye	64
Like a Jazz Song	65
Little Buddha Café	66
Faith	68
Restless II	70
Lima	72
Still	74
The Places I've Prayed II	75
The Places I've Prayed III	76
Las Calles	77
Run the World	78
Wild and Wired	80

Restless 4	82
Dead Sea	84
Now I Can Tell	86
Hate	89
Forgiveness	91
This Is It	92
Super Human	94
Love Her Fiercely	96
Stretch	97
Flow	99
A Day	100
Landing	101

Writing Right

I have not found a word

true enough

paper

thick enough

breath

full

enough

I have made stories with the ballpoint of my foot

but I cannot stay stationary

enough

to write

this

down

It is all so up

So transcendent of what it inspires

So life so love so live

It is sublime

It is not straight nor rhyme

It is not right

nor to be written

All that can't be put in word

in oration

in tongue

in lips

That which

never sits

still

enough
to grab
its tale

I have not written
recently
It
is busy righting
me

Culture Shock

You have landed
All that you know is yourself
Soon that too will change
Your sweat smells different from all the spice-filled food
Your practical sneakers- wet from monsoons
You do not speak the language
You
are foreign
Your reference points are nowhere on this map
All that you know is now all that you lack
There is no going back
You have landed
but have yet to find the ground
You are dumbfounded
as in
you have found out you are dumb
that the world is actually filled
mostly
with things you do not know
and at this moment
these things are right
and you are left
to figure it all out
and figure a way in.

Restless

My bed in India
was narrow
5 feet short
with a foot board
so feet could not hang
The only
"comfortable"
way to rest
was chest down
extremities spread
straddling
between rest
and restless

Sleeping is not easy
for the traveler
When rest is second
and less is first
when what you need is not sleep
nor pillow
nor snore
Any open door is suitable for storing the body after dark
and light is always lurking
and you welcome it with open arms
so you are always wide
awake
You put your rest at stake
for the sake
of all
the rest

The Places I've Prayed

Between Haridwar and Rishikesh
on a bus
swaying in Hindu Puja and Punjabi
with water to waist
suitcase soaked
and scared
I prayed
Pressed eyelids shut
Shit fuck this is it
I am going to die
in the Ganga River and monsoon
under moon and masala
I think I prayed to Krishna with Kabala
or Buddha
or Brahman
Don't remember, but I prayed
hard and heartfelt
Prayed to feel the ground again
to not go in such a place
so far from home

Why I Didn't Write Home

If home is where the heart is
my heart
is a circular argument around the equator
I don't discriminate against borders and
I get bored with order
so my heart is meant for backpacking
with a fishing rod spine and bate for lips
I make my way
A house doesn't give me any living room
I am most at free in the forest where
the trees praise my growth and
the grass admires my roots
I am somewhere between a nomad
and not mad when I am no one
when the wind juggles me in the palms of its hands
between the spice of masala and the
off beat
of samba-
I am home
So I will travel to these places where I am so surrounded
that I am completely alone
Travels that don't come equipped with a map
where the roads still aren't built and
the locals give you crap
Don't ask them what time it is
because its always right
to move in the unknown with confidence
and the largest grin

to sit still and taste the history in your food

to run after trains and rivers

to fall

into the arms of a jungle

to sleep

in the sand to watch the sun set

in a stranger's eyes

on a strange beach

with strange cheap beer

to bargain with the fear of being lost

to always unwrap the presence of

now

to let

and to go

So

I didn't write home

because it didn't feel right

I was somewhere dancing salsa or on a flight

in a bar on a back road

in a backwoods backwards town

never planning

to come back.

Hopeful Romantic

Not knowing what to do or what to say
because both would mean nothing
within the vastness of a day
We try to capture
film and photo and stories told
forgeries made of sugar and salt
flavors dissolved in the mouth of time
like beliefs we forget
or waves goodbye
water erasing sand
butterflies that die young
a youth we are never quite done with
wrinkles warranted
bodies lived in
Oh how romantic the smell of wine tasting and trouble
cigarettes after quitting
these breaths you'll never get back
days you cannot keep
even though they're yours
This is the most romantic part of all

The Travelers

My beliefs are frequent travelers

always packed and ready to go

always waiting to open a door

and run somewhere knew

They will sometimes travel aimlessly

or be lost

They are always up and antsy

looking to change their clothes

to see if they can walk in another's shoes

My beliefs have no sense of self

no shelf with their name engraved

They have no sense of home

and roam the streets

with a closed mouth and open fears

My beliefs are full suitcases

that never rest their case

a wet tongue about to taste

but they never swallow

My beliefs will never pretend to be certain

they are often circular

more than two sided

and rarely square

My beliefs

are never sure of themselves enough to brag

and they always beg the question

enough that it must

ask itself again

Think About It

I think
how the world does not
It does not know
it does not make promises
it does not decide
the world does not talk it through
it feels
This world is a feeling world
it doesn't make up its mind
it knows
and expands and moves towards the sun because it feels warmth
it feels gravity and breath and movement
the universe flows
because it feels
and it knows the most
more than the mind we try to master
it knows how to let go and move on
it knows how to circle back without grudge
it moves without eagerness and with ease
the universe doesn't ask
nor assume
it feels where there is movement and catches it
effortlessly and for free
fluidly fearlessly
all through feeling
or so I think

Cup of Tea

Listen closely to the kettle

a steaming whisper before the whistle

then

then

turn the fire off

before it announces itself too loudly

before it needs time to cool down

before it has potential to burn your mouth

Baby

let me blow this candle before the wax hits the table

before the kettle embarrasses the kitchen

before the plane descends

I don't like the sound of too much excitement

when it's bound to be over

when I am here only for a layover

before my next cup of tea

and I don't love you like you love me

Just temporarily we were simmering and

you weren't listening when I told you

I told you baby

I forewarned you that

I go

alone

and you can't come along and

I don't fall and

never fail to fold the hand

before the risk is too high

but you

love to play with fire
the sound of a screaming kettle before it blows
but boy
you ain't buoyant when the water boils and
you can't swim to shore if you aren't sure how to swim
so
dim the lights
before the lights go out

Express Train

Headphones in eyes on screen

Don't hear

don't see

Don't actually be where you actually are

How uneventfully filled it is with real things and their people

chitchat

And chewing

Laughter too young and too loud

Idiots

on the same train as you

Pretending like they're making connections

pretending like they have somewhere else

to be

Killing Time

I am digging up all the time I've killed

and asking it for forgiveness

trying to revive it

made a mistake

and killed time

caught between a long line and limbo

before letting go

after being left

you were right

time

when you ran out

left every

thing

didn't even pack

light

just ran out the back door

empty handed

no plans

just presence

The last time

you ran out, time

I turned and watched

the souls of your feet lifting as you ran through the door

you were rushing

to conclusion

an illusion

due east

I followed you
'round the corner
but eventually lost track of time

you are so good at leaving things behind
and letting go

Last time
I promised you
it would be the last,
time
I'd kill you
yet I am standing at your burial ground
once more
with a shovel
and a sorry
burying you
in coffins made of clocks
sometimes I sit there
wait and
watch
but
you never decompose
I guess there is no time
for wasting

Pack light

Your hostel

is nearing empty

and the beach

full of rain

and a table for one

seems lonely

and the stranger is all too strange

so take out the light you packed

outshine this misplaced

darkness

as soon as it appears

pack light

for days like this

and

carry on

Dear Tomek

I sent you a postcard from Malaysia
But I don't think you got it
I was unsure of the address scribbles
you wrote
quickly
on the back of my ticket out
of London
and I likely sent my letter to a hill top in Austria
miles from where you reside
But in this short postcard
I say
it was great to meet you
and I hope we cross paths again
The likelihood of this crossing
is slim
but the breath of our encounter was thick
and I pray this poem reaches you
across the wide seas

I approached you in St. James Park
You were smiling
too
at the duck walking
waddle
web foot
in the green
You were beaming light
wearing harem pants

an odd haircut
pony tail
in the center of your crown

You seemed strange enough to not consider me stranger

I asked where you were from
and you responded full
of life and love
and we sat under an old tree
for hours
and spoke about the world
and spirit
harmony
and grass
ground
the roundness of the earth

We made sense of it all
for a moment
and I considered it a miracle
that we met

When I left
for my train back to Charlton
you kissed my forehead
and said I have a traveler's soul
I hugged you tightly
like I had known you for lives

and said
confidently
I would see you soon

Soon has passed
and our paths may never cross again
But I am grateful
for the duck and the old tree
and to witness
a kindred spirit
wonder and wander through the
webbed foot
wideness
of the world

Brother

I heard his anguish
a rasp in his inflection
a tale through his bones
bothered and bottomless and beloved brother
you said it right and all and I felt it
how?
how did the words come in time?
how did the emotion fit itself into tongue and sound?
there's certainly something to savor in saying it full
emotive and almost ugly
authentic and aching
brother
I wish to say it right like you
to share the tug of lore
the laughter of loneliness
the hurry in my stillness
how can I archive this liveliness
this bearing witness
who will feel it sensitively
who will see it brightly
brother
bold and battle-cried and a broken voice that's beautiful
I wish to find the words for the wonder and wingspan of consciousness
of carrying on and letting go
How it's precious and how it's wretched
all wrapped in one

Missing Out

Aaron's eyes
are wide blue
like the ocean between him and his family
He misses home
Holds all that he had in a heavy empty
invisible bag on his back
He thinks he is off track
That there's a road waiting for his feet somewhere
That he is lost in limbo between the sweetness of moms cooking
and independence
He misses his dog
He misses American sarcasm
He misses the familiar brands of beer
and peanut butter
sticking to his bottom lip
He misses hip-hop.

So Aaron goes home
over the wide blue ocean between him and his family
Goes to his childhood bed
in his childhood home
to a living room
with all the room he needs for living.

Oh, the things he will be missing.

Shipwreck

Sink
or swim
or
sink your teeth into it
chew it up and spit it out alive

also floating is an option

Queso Fresco and Paneer

The traveler knows
you cannot expect things to be the same
things will contradict and confuse, amuse to no end
Things will move as they wish and not often at your pace
wisdom is learning to choose battles and try
to surrender happily
A smile
goes a long way
Especially
when you've lost your way
your tongue
your sense of direction
and sense of semantics
Cultural difference is not ornamental
It is deeper than garb and how to take your coffee
Good coffee is hardest to find where it's grown
You are never too grown to keep growing
Plan long layovers
rarely check the time
never check a bag
The best way to know a city is to walk it
Second best is to eat it
Third
write it a poem and make love to a local
dialect
know that no one
is stranger
than you

Roxanne

It's good to leave
good things
behind
Where the traveler keeps their
high school prom dress
old ballet shoes
and middle school friends

Boston never felt like home until I didn't live there
When I was too busy getting on my way
Yet as we stood in your kitchen
laughing part blunt part nostalgia
I realized why I always come back to you
and how I am always able to leave again

Friends who drop you off at the airport
and don't know when you will return
but trust you will come back better
with stories just for them

And the hugs get stronger
when it's been so long
so far
I love you more
the more I am not here
because when I come back
with my bags halfway still packed
and we sit on your porch

in cold air
longer hair
with different lovers than before
there's nothing between us
and there never will be
You get me
with the base of where I come from
and who that has turned into now
I love you for being my welcome home
for reminding me it is home
and that it's good to leave
such good things behind

Backpackers

I'm a collector
of single
serving
friends

find them
between baggage claim
open mics
salsa nights
books stores
and bucket lists

Friends that too
find comfort in the limbo
of a bus station

in the big picture
and the small talk

Friends that can verify
you saw the tips of Kashmir
the foothills of the Himalayas
that you
in fact
danced ballroom with that bartender in Rome

Witnesses of your adventure
who shared the lines to the Vatican

daring tan lines in Brazil
who know the thrill of your eyes
and shrill of your excitement

Friends who help make home of hostels
Who remind you
traveling alone
doesn't mean lonely

These friends are as real
as the rest
and I fondly remember their faces
their accents
their backpacks
and few of their names

Felipe

Let's take a trip

The wind had forgotten the texture of my hair

Let's leave

Catch

the next train to the next town

over

whelmed

with departure and arrive

somewhere new

that we have never known

Let's lose our watches and

wander with wonderlust

Trust

me

Let's

rent a car

go far

fetched

Let's leave

lover

friend

Lend

me your hands

for the day

Lose

our sense of direction

slow up and

hurry down

I'm making my way 'round the world

Don't

latch yourself to my hip just

lick my lips today

got to be on my way

more

earth

that needs to meet my feet

fears

I need to face and you're

head

over

heels

Just

travel with me

Unravel within me

today

Let's lie at the shore

watch the waves kiss the sand

goodbye

Leave

without

a word.

Maracuja

I never knew passion fruit
was more than a flavor
of candy and punch
at the corner store
more than
manufactured
made up
miscellaneous
'merica

Off the coast of Rio
with locals, capoeira, and sun
a tree taught me
spontaneity
dropped me
um milagre
em minhas mãos

I stared
stunned with stupidity
studied the soft
supple yellow
ripened richness
nested naturally
in my palms

"É um maracujá
dos deuses das árvores
Comê lo"
the wise ones said to the white

So I pressed
and parted
and bit
and slurped
savoring salivated
sticky satisfying
sssssllllltttthhhhwp
of gooey
golden
sweet sour tart
fruity
miracle
from the Isla Grande gods

In the company of sun and strangers
I surrendered to a smile
that was as big as the island
that was as wide as awake
holding passion
tightly on my tongue
tied
tasting like I was new again
yielding like the world was wiser
then
and there
under a tree
hidden in the company
of sand
and serendipity

Orange You Glad

This morning I ate an orange

Slowly

On purpose

A practice of listening closely

of offering my full attention

I peeled the orange at first with habit and rush

breaking the skin ungracefully

Then I stopped

and considered This Orange

The one in front of me

dripping in my palms

I paused in presence and

started to peel politely

waiting for the peel to consent

I tasted the sweet, sour, tingling tart, taut and supple taste

The skin

the slurp

I heard and felt

each

one at a time

and then

all at once

I wanted to memorize the moment

as it unraveled into magic and mystery

This moment that was mine

but didn't belong to me

that I could not control

could only watch and feel and try to show up for

This Orange

organically grown from tree, sun, and evolution

I wanted to take a picture

but knew it was fleeting

a feeling to be forgotten

forever

only ever

to exist here and now

A moment of mouthful

mindful

flavorful

and alive

Hangry

I woke up hangry
In need of sunshine
and sunny-side eggs
bread
with butter
and old school jams
I woke up hangry
missing Philly
and cinnabuns
coriander
and chai
Missing 21 and high
In need of some soul food
Low mood
High strung
Hangry
Need to
break
fast
quick
I be buggin' bedside
before breakfast
cant come fast enough
Feed me Feed me
Feed me morning
I have slept in patience
and am ready
to be fed and full

Recipe for Disaster

You taste

good

Like an apple

fresh from tree

Like beer

batter

cinnamon

almond

velvet cake

coated

icing

enticing pearl

dropped

love

I ought to swallow you whole

like nectar in the back of my throat

sweet

sugar cane between my teeth

You are like something from a tree

ripened

full

healthy

lively and bright

You taste like chocolate coated nights

and spliffitos

platanos y almendras

Querida Vitamina,

quiero tragarte completo

como la luna presta la luz del sol

You be like sol food

and good for soul

Sweetness and powerful

food for thought

You taste good

like forbidden fruit

baked

and sugared

Sugar,

honey,

You taste

like a strong morning sun and

cup of coffee

like coco oil and lips

sips of wine

sangria

tea

peach

You taste like an orchard

marinated in sun

taste buds blossomed

Something grown from the roots up

You taste like

something I want to cook up for dinner

Whole food

fair trade

spice mixture

season

crave

Babe

let me make a pie of you

bake a cake

a platter

lather you in buttered bacon

and go ham

You taste

damn

good

like spanish between our tongues

like a language, new

aprendiendo la forma de tu boca

Lléname con tu sabor

árbol

algo

de aire y alimento

fresh from tree

something I would pick

Lick your lips

and tell me

how I

feed you

A Good Find

Encuéntrame
en la esquina de
las escaleras
y la roca
con la vista buenísima
de aventura y alpaca
de yoga y waychuma
of whistles and wonder
Encuéntrame aqui
buscando, respirando
cerca a los nubes
con newness and witchcraft
with Reiki
breathing between space
of mountain and sky
A town made of wool and mystics
of shamanism, Tao, and clay
where there is play in dance
and light in all our crowns
How did we all get here
perfectly on time
with a dime, dos soles
and unconditional love
Como hemos llegado
envueltos en amor y canela
en palo santo y alegría
en el espacio de ofrecer
con el poder de curar
con manos y mágica
y tiempo

11,000 feet

Bring me to a house of healing

To a circle circulating

Listening

Ear

Drums

Humming

Birds

Chimes

in

out

of body

but all my skin

Hold me Cuzco

from pachamama to wiraccocha

In the arc of my iris

Remind me to close all three eyes

and open my heart

that to each their om

Cuzco, brillo

Bring me to the medicine

growing in mountains

Help me peak

Shock my chakras

Unlock my dharma

Show me my karma carried in consciousness

Show me sunset in stone

la luz

my home

Remind me of the family I have never met
and all there is to let and
go
Cusco
call me back
and back
again
and again

Sacred Space

Find peace in Pisac
Perch on a porch and watch
the hummingbirds love the trees
Watch the trees love the wind
and the wind love the chimes
Take time
to unwind and decompress
post stress and pre the rest
Sit in limbo
long and listen
Find peace in
suspension
between your breath
Don't test
the waters just
be fluid and free
Surrender to the
truth of what connects
you to the trees
and the trees to the birds
and the birds to the wind
Chime in
Take time
Let time take
you
in
between the breath
of its wings

the wonder of breeze

Find freedom in this space

unlaced and unsure

Find peace in Pisac

perched

where the mountains hold sacred space

and the clouds come in to

sit and

watch

Go

My alpaca wool blanket
black pleather jacket
and beloved poncho

I decided to let it all go
Easier left than loved
Leave things behind where they belong
Put them to rest
Move on
Let go
Be light
Don't be afraid to pack less
Bring only what you need
Need less
Need less to say,
to do,
to wear,
to fear
Let it all go
Or Rather
let it all stay
and you go

Moving On

This time was easy
To leave
Didn't care
Didn't cry
Didn't carry anything out
Left all I had bought or borrowed
All the friends or enemies I made
Decided
it all had its time
temporary or trite
and moved
the fuck
on

This time was easy
when the town
was drought dry
and I was ready for the next
Ready for the new
for the different
To be present with a place
perfect
for not yet knowing my name
Start out plain and blank and
fill it all in
again
from scratch
This time was easy

to detach

to move out

and not look back

Fed up

Just left

and it was right

so right

to move the fuck on

The Rush

There's this fear

that if I slow down

 I won't get it all done

But when I slow down

there's less to do

More to enjoy

to laugh to savor

to be with

Isn't that living?

Isn't living the smelling and the chew?

Is it not so much a moment of pause and ponder?

What are you rushing for?

Life is too short to rush through it quickly

Too much of an uneven trail to run straight and flat to the finish line

You may even enjoy pausing to take rocks out of your shoe

You're allowed to stop just for the view

just to feel the rush

of stillness

Allow

If you let me
I will love you
Like soil loving grass
Like supporting your growth towards the sun
I will lend you the Reiki in my palms
The power in my core
grant me permission
and I will love you
all and up and wide
Clear as glass
breakable as bend
I will love
Arms wrapped around the width of your earth
My love
Let me share me
with you
teach you my skin
Sensitive and kind
My gaze gripped
My goddess guided
My love
Let me give you this love that I have charged in light
And promise it forever
like the moon

Let me love you
alive and alert
mindful and meaningful
and never mine

Love Me

Love me
like unison and ukulele
Like lips locking
in language learning
Love me like
morning coffee
cacao and coca
Like leaves
for Inti and pachamama
Love me like sabiduría de ayahuasca
Like siesta midday
Like you love to say
what is
and nothing more
Love me like this
is something more
Something continent
Something ocean
Something sky
Love me high and ground
Love me to core and mantle
and crust
Love me
trust
Like I know you must
Babe
Love me
like it counts
With third eye

on all fours
with five senses
and seven chakras
Love me in your crown, king
Sing me
like I am song
with spinal chords
sharp
Like this be major
Like this is key
Like this is sound
Love me loudly
Musically
Naturally
Like wave and shore
Like you are sure
Love me in the lines of your palms
Show me your hands
Convince me
Quick
I'm questioning the risk of my rising heart
and the deep deep depth of the fall
Love me like Fall
in Boston
and Spring
in step
Like there's nothing less
Like you feel me in your chest
Chico
Rico

Love me rich

Love me twitch and taste and tall

Love me

water

fall

wet

Love me let

Love me go

Love me sex that curls your toes

Love me whole and holistic

Like a mouth full of ommm

Love me like I am home

Like I am rest stop

Like I am restless

waiting

for a sign

from you

Dying for you

to love me

like I love life

with you.

Go on

Go on

Go

Play your ukulele

Sing me those songs

that were written

by someone

in love

Affirmation

Do you see your Self?

multifaceted

dimensional

dynamite

de estrellas

damn

dynamic

dame

Like Rumi say

You are not just a drop of Ocean

You are all the ocean in a drop

Did you see your oceanic Self this morning?

Manifested from sea to skin

full of the world

and wild

and wonder, woman?

Lake Water Calm

Love quietly
calm
and still
Do not rush the heart
while it tries
to hammock
Hold gently
as if to heal
as if hands are heel
grounded in genesis
This is something special
careful not to spill it
nor spell it out
Withhold definition
hold with listen
hear the heart out
before you reel him in
it might not be real for him
yet
Don't hope
it won't happen more if you do
Just love
quietly
like lake water calm
like late night palms
are still

Loving Me

You never loved me
Enough
Was too tough to feel
All I could be felt for
I never knew I could love so deep and stupid
So life long and short
I never knew I could be naive enough
To love a man who could not love me back
knew from the beginning
This was all me
That our love to you was light
And our love to me was hearted
I gave my all
To a man with one hand out
And the other raised in question
too high for me to reach
How embarrassing
unrequited
And riveting
Front row seats nail biting
Story of a broken heart
What karma
What kill
What cold

I could only call my mother when it ended
Cried into her love for me
That was warm and full

That had no doubt I was worthy of
Both hands out
She held me through the phone
Loving me
As much as I could be loved

The Hum of Home

I want to tell my mother
that she is hummingbird
that she is the song of something
of wings and whispers
I want to tell her I believe
she is the rollover wisdom
from my past lives

I want her to know
that I never want to
see her go
and I remember vividly
the moment
I realized she would
and I have cried on this truth's behalf
ever since

I want to tell my mother that she
is gold
and purple maroon
and radiant
and light
skin
and bold bones
that she is chicken pot pie and gluten free crusts
apple sauce and
echinacea
cinnamon

fork ridged cucumbers
and red wine
challah
healing
hands and
hips
and her teeth
so lucky to never leave her smile

I want her to know
she taught me
the importance of the moon
and of a letter
of kindness
and mindfulness
and gestures
She has taught me unconditional love
and how special I am

I want my mother to know
that she is the first place I lived
so she will
always be my home

I want my mother to know
that she is hummingbird
that she is something natural and musical and kind
that she is so much more than
my

mother
She is a master
of much
and marinated in light
and I have tried many of times to write her
a poem
and none suffice

You cannot write
how she
is rice
and breath
caution
and strength
how she is lavender and grace
touch
and warmth
how she is great
and ground
and giving
goddess
full of focus

She is freedom in spine
and wine in shelf
happy and health
and the hum
of home

Mourning Walks

Dad,
You need to not worry
that we will cry in despair
That your absence will turn us all to alcohol and awful
I promise
I will cover all mirrors
rip my clothes
sit Shiva
I'll host a poker tournament in your honor
Probably write a book about how you knew the key to happiness
Happily name a daughter after you

You have no need to ask
that your death be dreadful
but more importantly
now
you should know
how I speak of you
my live
and well
and joyful father
How often I say
"I must credit my dad for that"
When asked how I am
 "never better"
Or told I look nice
"I am nice"

I brag regularly about how great you are
The Friday nights you dedicate to my mother
The time you commit to sick synagogue members
When I'm revered for my ability to pack light
I laugh and
in admiration explain
your thrift store packing methods.

I remember you now, constantly
In my stride and voice
In my choices to spend wisely
and save for adventures
In my desire to live big
and important
and for others
In my ability to rage for reason and what is right and just
Dad, you are something just so right and special
Something like an earthly Saint
Lively, smart, compassionate
loud and full of conviction
A presence that commands
A man who lives
by the words he speaks
and seeks truth

Dad,
I am lucky to have inherited
your habits for early rising
and restless legs

For an urgency to wake up
because we can sleep when we're dead
What a gift
to be a witness of your life
To watch you change into something same
but softer and with wiser eyes
To watch you age a body housed around a child's demeanor
You are aging agelessly
Untamed and handsome
Happy and hurrying to do it all
and do it right

Dad, you are right
You should know how we feel about you now
before the finish line
You should know that you are loved
100 times behind my back
and your memory will live on
in my anatomy and anecdotes

Dad,
You will die doing what you love
because you love to do it all
But I promise I won't say it
I won't soften the blow
Won't try to ease the pain
of your demise
I will cry and cry and cry a pond
with a morning walk's worth of circumference

And I'll wake up every dawn to mourn
I will move briskly
with a bounce in my heels
with a pride of being yours
thinking about how wonderful you are
much like I do now

Forever 21

We try on unicorn headbands
and listen to Brittany Spears
talk about our bellies and our breasts
my love of bralletes
her - lateral stripes
We laugh at the high-heal boots
she ditched back at the car
We choose comfort over look
but never miss a chance to catch our own reflection

I hate shopping
except with my grandma
We usually buy nothing but time
pretending to be younger than we are
We prance around amongst the crop tops and tween girls
with too many holes in their jeans
pretending to be worn out and old

My grandma tells me how she's seen it all before
The bell bottoms and bodysuits
fringe and furs
She knows something I cannot
having witnessed the recycling of time
We delight in the things that have changed with age
and the things that never will
Like lighthearted laughter
and listening

We know

we don't have all the time in the world

so we have all the world in our time

Fill it with stories of both silly and sad

Soak it all up

like wrinkles wanting cream

She teaches me how to stay young

To be carefree and sometimes careless

We hug and kiss and girlishly

galivant around the store

Pretending we are 21

Pretending all moments don't die young

Wishing it were forever

Red Eye

Fly in the direction of the sun

East

Towards India and calm

Plane painted pink and purple streak

like a slim street

made of horizon and a homeland

that is not yours

but still so sweet

like jubilee and honey

sticky situation

trying to find home when it is nowhere

only en route

only in fly

in walk

in wander

In the direction of the sun

Like a Jazz Song

Listening to samba music
as I speak in broken Hindi with my auto wallah
on my way to meet my Greek friend for Chinese food
before practice with my Afghani salsa partner
in New Delhi, India…

He wants to charge me
50 extra rupees
because of traffic.
"Bahiya…
Hamesha traffic hota hai!"
"There's always traffic" in Delhi
Always too much that things move slow
A chaos that's electric
and overcharged
Something like a jazz song
chaotic yet collected
It's hard to give directions here
To speak straight about a place
so out of line
to hear screeching horns like music
 to sing along with an offbeat accent
asking your lips to learn this language
your tongue to learn the flavors
to accept the cacophony and chaos
because it's okay
to be a little
overcharged

Little Buddha Café

I was mid swing
eleven motorbike miles
north of Delhi
and a hemisphere away
from shore
He tells me
he would soon return home
and not leave outside
a 3 mile radius
for a year
or two
until
he was
still
enough
to know the movement
instilled
around him

and in a moment
I overstood
that I mustn't always run
or spin
swim
or train hop
frantic
to fly
that stillness

is still required
to know movement

And as quickly as I learned
I forgot
And went on my way

Faith

Auntie told me to pray to her guru
that I didn't believe in
A shrine
embellished in reds and golds and glitters
frames with faces
of the gods and the greats
that guide her

I was crying in broken Hindi and heart
when Auntie said
to pray for protection
from her guru
to make myself a believer
line my forehead
with alien alter
filled with a faith
that I didn't deserve
that I was too white to warrant
too wasteful too doubtful
too distressed damsel

but there she was
offering me her faith
assuring me in her faith
feeling it for me
lending me her gods
her glitter her gold her greats
and guidance

so I prayed

to something

with a face

and no name to me

repeated something in broken Hindi

and broken heartedly cried

to her guru

asked her guru

prayed to her guru

had faith in her guru

until I let something go

until my heart weighed less

until I was less

than something

I did not even know

that I did not even believe

Restless II

A yoga mat
and a Sharper Image mini pillow
on the second floor of Lima's airport
Bridging the petite indoor tree
and a French girl
I slept
Not really
Interrupted by arrivals
midnight floor waxing
and fluorescent light
Just one more flight away
from destination

I ate an empanada de pollo
con limon
a perfect Peruvian nighttime snack
Chatted with the French girl
about the realities we land at
in between the highs of traveling
The less than luxurious
layovers
the stress of losing
time differenced by
the zones we hop

These moments
are so much of traveling
she said

without complaining

I agreed

plainly

with a small

sleepy smile

and the taste of midnight in my mouth

Lima

Late

And

Lonely

I am missing home

In a hurry to leave limbo

Lately

having a hard time telling time

when time is telling me

urgently

a surge in me

to live loudly with

longevity

Lately

Lima

I have been lonely

Trying to hold still

hold tight

hold on

and catch my breath

with just two hands

Its hard

when daylight is outside

playing in a language

you do not know

and you forgot to pack your favorite pair of jeans

but there's light at the end of Lima
after the tunnel of clouds
gives up for the day

Still

I watch the ocean meditate

returning to shore

again and again

I remember

the movement of a drum

and a conversation

about settling down

in a three

mile radius

to find movement in your surrounding

to sit

on a front porch

where you can't look back

and to be moved

by stillness

The Places I've Prayed II

I think it was hormones

But nevertheless

I was crying

Deep

In my sternum deep

Needing love and light

and guidance crying

in my small sublet room in Cusco

on a rough red carpet

high up in the mountains

I needed something to remind me I wasn't alone

So

I got on my knees

Palms pressing

Holding the smallest bit of faith I had

I prayed

To some standard concept of God

Like a being in the sky type God

Like answer my prayers I surrender type God

Asking why and how and when?

The Places I've Prayed III

In the same red rugged apartment bedroom
post sunrise yoga
pre cajon jam session
in the middle of the day
at the edge of my bed
the bottom of my breath
I pressed
my palms holding faith
full
I said thank you
for the space and time
for the making of music
and love
lessons
of this life
I said thank you for the now
and there was no need to know why

Las Calles

These streets are women
wagging their tales
Tandapata of trips and stone
dogs roaming with dim light
jewelers with crystals
men with loose eyes
walls with no mouths
Here
the streets are feminine
las calles son femininas
laced with ayahuasca and cho-ku-rei
the streets are feminine here
where our walks warrant whistles
and fear wakes up as the sun goes down
women women we are the streets
las calles
las son femininas
these streets are feminine
irony caught in the concrete
curl
of a dead end

Run the World

Si tu no ya sabes
Yo soy la quien te va a decir
Que el mundo
de mágico y loco y more than we can chew
es el tuyo
Tu, chica linda
de charla y choclo
de chocolate y café
multigrain for breakfast babe
The woman who runs the streets swims the rivers
bikes the hills
How how how do you not see
that the world IS your finger tips
It is your purple lips and laughter of light and freedom
Amiga mejor
de cerveza y sabiduría
de cool
Tan fucking cool chica
Esto es
This is it
El mundo para ti mujer
The world for your making and taking
Take it
The trip
triathlon
trail run
the title, take todo
Todo fucking todo
and translate it into yours
Es el tuyo
Te juro amiga

quien me ha dicho "Hazlo"
Te digo sin duda
"Do it!"
Grab it like a goal and don't let go 'til you get it
Deus damnit
Chica
Goddess of flannel and hips
of hipster and hater
Sarcastic soulful sassy warrior
go for it
Whatever "it" is
You already have it growing in your hair
and heart
Your world is your hungry hands
Own it
Hone it
And I promise to remind you de vez en cuando
y encontrarte por donde andes
en este mundo increíble
de miedo y milagros
de propósito y próximos
Y si sea más de lo que puedas masticar
hazlo con tu boca abierta
ojos anchos
Leave a mess
un desastre
por todos tus deseos
por que
Because
I wanna watch you run the world

Wild and Wired

Don't wait
Good things will come
to those
who urgently
eagerly
maybe even impatiently seek
Go
Do
Be
Ask
What are you waiting for?
Besides the thing you're waiting for..
The thing is
it's waiting for you
Who told you that your time will be replenished?
Who told you there's a reason to wait?
Aren't you wondering?
Aren't you wild and wired?
Aren't you made mad by this mystery and magic, man!?
It's magic, maniac
It's a miracle, don't you see?

Write it down
quick
Live it up
fast
Hurry like you only have an hour to live
like you'll never get the next hour back

Your breaths are running out
and there's no take backs
no do overs
Good things will come to those who create
who throw caution to wind
and wind down only after winding it all the way up
until they're spinning in music
Make it happen
Stand your ground
Give a fuck
Give a shit
Fuck it, give two
Give too much
Lose it loosely
Shoot for the stars
Love to the moon and never look back
Don't wait
Don't be wishful
Be mouthful be arms full
full-hearted and hurried
Have your cake
Eat it too
Have seconds
because it's just a matter of minutes
a day
a year
a lifetime
awaits you

Restless 4

You've been hired by the night
to keep the secrets of dusk and dawn
Do not try to sleep
By all means
sleep when you do
but don't fight with the gift of awake
You've been given the extra hours that they speak of
You've been given the "if only more time in a day" they're dreaming of
You are the dream with eyes open in the dark
seeing what few can feel
knowing what few will know
Do not fight your mattress to hold you better
You are the one who holds
Do not fight the bold of restless legs
You need less rest
Rest assured- never
but don't fight it
Keeper of the night
nesting between dusk and dawn
Damn the eyes sagging and swollen
agitated and sugar sucker for sweets
You have all the time you need and more than you could dream of
Make the most of the magic, knight
Don't make light of the dark
Watch it closely
Capture it and cook it up for breakfast
Fast

Quick

Stop counting sheep

Zees are last for a reason

Dead Sea

At the lowest point on earth
you will float
Saturated with silt and salt
A sea
Dead and daring to the punctures and cuts on your cuticles
Lather yourself in wet earth
Make a mud mask
Mucky and dry
quickly in the sun
Walk on crystals
Soles stabbing against the salted sand
Lie back and bask
Bake in body of water heavier than you
Look at the mountains
making space
making sunsets
The closest to gravity you'll get
Confront it
and you will float

At your lowest point
you must float
Even if you fight it, it's all that you will do
Surrender to salt
stay still
soft
enough
that you are held by something

that slips through fingers

At your lowest point
you are buoyant
you are held
You mustn't hurry or it will hurt
You must let the dirt seep deep until it dries
You must lie with the mountains silver lining the edges

Go lower than the level of the sea
where most things are dead
and you will feel how alive you are
and the only way to go
is up

Now I Can Tell

I love him

I know it

Mostly I feel it

The way my eyes narrow and my gut gathers when I see him

The way my parts twinge and my thoughts get all hopeful when I hear his voice

I can tell

I can tell I love him

And so I might tell him maybe

Tell him I have always and that I just needed forever

tell him I know I hurt him but I'm a healer

I will tell him we were made for this

That the backs and the forths were momentum for a lifetime of loving him madly

Baby

I know you need time

Take it

I know you need power

Assert it

I mean it

Never meanly

Mi amor

My love

Who speaks my language and knows how to listen as good as he licks

A tongue made of Romance

and mango

A man made of castles and curls

How can I tell him I love him surely and more than ever?

That this time is the last time
third time's the charm
you're the one
I've counted
I've consulted my best friends and my mother
Consensus is
you're the love of my life
and I'm yours
It's true
I can tell
I can tell it
and I hope to tell it til you hear it and open your heart for me again
I understand hesitation and not wanting to hurt
I respect your reservations and revere your righteousness
Just know
my hands are ready when you are
I've been honing how to hold you
like a harvest
Waiting for the right amount of sun
and managing my hunger
I promise I am ready now
patient but eager to please you
To witness you waking and
worry about losing you
To watch you never go gray
and get greater with age
I can tell I love you
because I feel scared to say it
But I can tell it

I have to tell you

Loudly and with lust and lure

Que me escuches

Que no me dudes

Just hold the hand I have left open just for you

Hate

ooo how quickly this love turns to venom
killed you with kindness
and now wanting to kill
quickly stomach turns
jaw taught
shoulders locked
tongue loaded
and that love
becomes hatred
fuming frantic fucking hatred
The heat and the hopelessness
fiery rage
torturous hate
hot
like it's hurrying to hell
and doesn't know how to heel
I thought this time
it wouldn't turn tragic
wouldn't become bitter or hard to bite
But so bad we are at being, baby
boy
bastard
Who's such a bitch to battle
and wears armor when I'm bare naked and needing healing
Where does the love and this hatred meet or mesh
Where does breath of fresh air become despair and disdain
How did we do it all so wrong, darling
Damnit damn you I hate you fucking hate you

for showing me your dark side
and calling on my demons
Devastated
full of doubt and dare
damned if I love you any more

and I will be damned

Forgiveness

Ahh
and then there's forgiveness
When the fiery rage caramelizes into something chewy and sweet

Oh the sweetness of surrender
of each lesson and its teacher

The gritty gratitude
like salt cleansing open wound
Like pain is a practice of patience and purifying

When all the crying subsides
eyes puffy
heart hollow
hands hurting from holding on
too exhausted to find hope
Here
the healing
has already happened
and forgiveness is there
waiting for you to stop fighting
to stop forgetting
You've felt it
All of it

And now you're free

This Is It

Just a bunch
of little bits
of this
Try not to blink
Don't breathe too fast
Can't breathe too full
Feel it all fully
Smell taste touch talk to it listen
Memorize it and make it meaningful
Whatever it is
That's all that it is
A bunch of bits of just that
Like the Billowing of my sunflower dress
and knowing he's watching
Resplendent fall trees
hearing the crunch of leaves
Walking
with my cheek kissing his shoulder
Falling in love
Snowed in, curled on his lap while playing with his curls
and sun
Uhhhh the suuun
The thing you were made for and made from
And how it comes every single day
The daaaayyys
The hours
The minute details of the mundane
Handstands

Fiestas
Laughing with friends
Trends that fleet
Bare feet and holding his hand after missing him madly
The sky reflected in Sanctuary swamp
Coasting on my bike down beacon
Sharing popcorn and a pitcher con ellas
Light hearted conversations with strangers
So many strangers
and strange things and feeling estranged
That's all it is
A bunch of that
I'll take it
Whatever it is
Take it all in

Super Human

I am terrified

I am brave

I am confident

I am insecure

I am full of choices

Full of eagerness

Patiently waiting

to explode

My heart

is a loaded gun

My arms- bare

I am boundless

I have blind spots

I'm surrounded by mirrors

I know magic

I know

Manifest it make it matter

I am a matter of fact

An act of earthly intuition

I am emotion and thought

thoughtful and in theory

I am terrified

but really

I am brave

I can't be defeated on two feet

I can't be unarmed when I am my own army and war

I am grounded

I am focused

I am forgiving and funny enough

I am enough

I am complete

Carefree and cautious

Calm and storm

All in and full out

Outrageous and inspired

In it to win it and on top of the world

Aren't I free?

Aren't I spent?

Aren't I dying?

Aren't I alive?

Aren't we each all of it?

And isn't that super human?

Love Her Fiercely

No one can love me as good

as self loving self

How perfectly made I was to love everything I am

To embrace the details that some may call flaws

I know better

Of course

I am the closest to the source within me

And I love her fiercely

Fearlessly

Fully

Arms wrapped around her waist

Waiting for no one

To love me better

Stretch

if it's malleable

it will not break

it will bend

for the bold

and broaden for the bitter

your heart is a muscle

that should be stretched

make it limber

with love

let it laugh

a lot

light

heartedness

hardly

causes damage

let

it

go

loose

and it cannot tear

can't be tortured

don't tell it secrets

it will learn to hold on and whisper

always let it scream

so it never surrenders

to structure

stagnation is for the

statues

that crack over

time

that stay stoic

and sleepless

and know solitude

too well

Flow

Make sure to rest
between your rising
Let
after you go
Do
but then be

All grand things try less than it seems

This is flow

Ask the sun
that knows to set

Ask the ocean
that is hammocked by sand

Man, you don't have to try so hard
Try soft
Try supple

and see how powerful you'll become

A Day

Today was a butterfly
Short-lived and beautiful
Won't last long
Just dusk to dawn
Morning run to run down in the evening
Legs up the wall
Sighs out the mouth
What a day
One you will remember fondly
A day that felt alive and new and young
A day filled with laundry and dishes
wishes getting granted
Learning and loving
lollygagging on the phone
Today was a snowflake
Crisp, complete
one-of-a-kind
Made from sky
yet melted by its sun
Today is the sunflower
tilted towards the light
out my kitchen window
So full of direction
Today had direction
Today felt alive
Sun soaked
And flourish
Nourished from its morning cocoon
A day that flew by
until its beautiful, brilliant death

Landing

Now she is ready
for home
for bed sheets and blankets
a shelf full of tea
How long it has taken
to value the simplicity of a welcome mat
But she's ready now
to make a home
and make her bed in it
To paint walls
make roots
a routine
There is no place like home when you haven't picked one yet
Haven't chose
to be still enough
for long enough
to build a roof
Never lived
in these places
of paradise and parade
of far far away and near to heart
Never lived there long enough
to buy hooks
or hangers
Never hung around
long enough
to take off shoes
grab a chair

situated

between limbo

a bus stop

a backpacker

Bag packed light

but heavy hearted

It's time to make a home

she finally says

after a mouth full of foreign

and feet of forests

flourished and found

She is ready

for a spice shelf and

a shovel for the snow

because there's a place like home

ABOUT THE AUTHOR

Hannah Adams is a yoga teacher and poet based in Boston, MA. She was a finalist at the 2010 Women of the World Poetry Slam, representing Philadelphia while a student at Temple University. She graduated with a BA in Philosophy and an eagerness to learn new languages and live abroad. Her first book of poetry, *Written in the Last Year of My Teens*, was published in 2010.

After spending most of her twenties living between Asia and Latin America, Hannah naturally shifted from spoken word to written word poetry. Back in Boston, she now continues to write poetry, and also finds her creative voice while teaching yoga classes, using poetic language to guide her students through movement with breath.

To learn more about Hannah, you can visit her website: www.hannahadams.fit, follow her on Instagram: @hannahadamsyoga, and subscribe to her YouTube page: Hannah Adams Yoga.

www.ingramcontent.com/pod-product-compliance
Lightning Source LLC
Chambersburg PA
CBHW020917090426
42736CB00008B/671